June O'Sullivan
and Nick Corlett

# 50
## fantastic ideas for
# sustainability

FEATHERSTONE

FEATHERSTONE
Bloomsbury Publishing Plc
50 Bedford Square, London, WC1B 3DP, UK
29 Earlsfort Terrace, Dublin 2, Ireland

BLOOMSBURY, FEATHERSTONE and the Feather logo are trademarks of Bloomsbury Publishing Plc

First published in Great Britain, 2021 by Bloomsbury Publishing Plc

A catalogue record for this book is available from the British Library

ISBN: PB: 978-1-4729-8412-8; ePDF: 978-1-4729-8414-2

2  4  6  8  10  9  7  5  3  1

Designed by Lynda Murray

Printed and bound in India by Replika Press Pvt. Ltd.

To find out more about our authors and books visit www.bloomsbury.com
and sign up for our newsletters

# Contents

# Introduction

A central tenet of Early Years Education is to prepare children for undertaking their roles as responsible global citizens. With sustainability finally moving towards the centre of the political and public agenda, there is no better time to engage our toddlers and children in environmentally-friendly activities and learning. Nursery teachers, parents and carers play a big role in supporting children's first steps on their journeys to becoming responsible citizens.

Too often adults dismiss young children as too young to understand their role, but we disagree. Early education is a natural starting point for learning about the planet and children are much more competent and thoughtful than we give them credit for. Children as young as three can wield quite an influence once they understand the consequences of their behaviour. They can persuade adults to recycle, repair or repurpose more often. Children often challenge us in our nurseries, reminding us to turn off the tap and not waste water, actively collecting litter and pushing us to recycle our packaging not just at work but also at home.

The purpose of this book is to share activities that can help nursery teachers, parents and carers provoke conversations with children and with each other about making changes in our daily lives to help us become more responsible, respectful and actively engaged in the sustainability agenda. We are not asking anyone to become an eco-warrior, but small changes make a big difference.

Education is a very powerful pathway to sustainability, and as adults we can integrate sustainability into every element of our leadership, pedagogy and operational practice. Sustainability is not a subject or part of an environmental programme; it is central to the whole learning experience and needs to be part of a broad and inclusive quality education.

We are influenced by the principles of the concept of permaculture, which advocates living lightly on the planet and in harmony with nature to ensure we can sustain human activities for many generations to come. The seventeen Global Sustainable Development Goals were adopted by all United Nations Member States in 2015, as a shared blueprint for peace and prosperity for people and the planet, now and into the future. They include quality education, climate action and clean water (you can search for the full list online). The activities in this book are designed with these goals in mind.

## The eight 'R's

The eight 'R's are perfect for reminding us of what sustainable options are available, and we've used them to inspire the activities in this book. All the ideas are multi-layered and cross-curricular and use music, dance, arts, crafts, science and nature, narration and demonstration to introduce small children to sustainability in an engaging, fun and positive way. We do not have all the answers to sustaining our planet, but we will have greater success if we teach our children about their planet from the earliest age.

| 1 | Reduce | Decrease consumption and wastage of food, materials and resources. |
|---|---|---|
| 2 | Reuse | Use materials many times and for different purposes. |
| 3 | Repair | Fix things rather than discarding them or repurposing them. |
| 4 | Recycle | Be aware of alternatives to discarding rubbish and educate children on the importance and impact they can have through this. |
| 5 | Rot | Let things go back to the earth to enrich the next crop of plants while also providing a habitat for many insects and small rodents. |
| 6 | Respect | Nurture understanding of, and respect for, nature and natural processes and reduce the extent to which they are violated, showing consideration and compassion for people and animals. |
| 7 | Reflect | The habit or skill of being thoughtful and asking questions. |
| 8 | Responsibility | Be trusted to take care of something or to do something worthwhile. Be socially and economically sustainable, for example, by supporting fair trade and local markets. |

### The structure of the book

The pages are all organised in the same way. Before you start any activity, read through everything on the page so you are familiar with the whole activity and what you might need to plan in advance.

**What you need** lists the resources required for the activity. These are likely to be readily available in most settings or can be bought or made easily.

**What to do** tells you step-by-step what you need to do to compete the activity.

The **Health & Safety** tips are often obvious, but safety can't be overstressed. In many cases, there are no specific hazards involved in completing the activity, and your usual health and safety measures should be enough. In others, there are particular issues to be noted and addressed.

**Top tips** are helpful hints to make an activity work well and have been learned from experience!

**Taking it forward** gives ideas for additional activities on the same theme, or for developing the activity further. These will be particularly useful for things that have gone especially well or where children show a real interest. In many cases, they use the same resources, and in every case, they have been designed to extend learning and broaden the children's experiences.

**What's in it for the children?** tells you (and others) briefly how the suggested activities contribute to learning.

# Citrus peel shapes

**Reuse fruit peel**

## What you need:

- Citrus peels: lemons, limes or oranges
- Cookie cutter shapes
- Plastic sewing needle
- Twine
- A baking tray
- Heavy items: stones, big books, etc.

## What to do:

1. Remove any remaining fruit from the inside of the citrus peels. This will prevent them from going mouldy.

2. Cut the peels into smaller sections and then let the children make them into shapes using cookie cutters.

3. Place the peels on a flat surface and put the baking tray right side up on top. Fill the tray with the heavy items to flatten the peels and leave for 24 hours.

4. Remove the baking tray and invite the children to arrange the shapes into different patterns.

5. Using the plastic needle and twine, help the children thread through the middle of the peel shapes to make necklaces, decorations and so on.

### What's in it for the children?

This sensory-based activity allows children to develop and extend their fine motor skills as they handle and thread small objects. This activity reuses fruit peel that would otherwise be wasted.

### Taking it forward

- Turn the citrus peel into festive ornaments. Shape them, then leave them out to dry until completely hardened. Using the needle, place a ring of twine through the top and make a loop. They can be hung up around a room.

# Introduction to composting

Show how compost works

## What you need:

- An outdoor space with natural materials: grass, dried leaves, etc.
- An empty plastic bottle or glass jar
- Water
- A rubber band
- A small square of gauze

## What to do:

1. Start by going to an outdoor space and collecting different natural materials with the children: grass, dried leaves, etc. You could also ask the children to save any appropriate scraps from their lunches, such as apple cores or orange peel.

2. Place the children's collection into the bottle or jar and add a small amount of water for moisture.

3. Put the gauze over the top and secure it with a rubber band.

4. Observe the process of how the natural materials break down over time. This may take one to three months to happen, so position the bottle in a place where it won't be disturbed, such as on a windowsill.

5. Invite the children to go on a worm hunt and put the worms they find into the bottle or jar to help speed up the process. Keep the bottle out of direct sunlight and return the worms to their natural habitat afterwards.

### What's in it for the children?

This is a visual way of showing children how natural resources break down and release nutrients back into the earth.

### Taking it forward

- Ask the children to describe what they think might happen if instead they filled the bottle with plastic wrappers and rubbish.

- Use this activity as an opportunity to talk about rubbish and landfills.

### ✚ Health & Safety

When collecting natural materials with the children, ensure that the area is free from any dangerous debris or plants.

# Bottle planters

Indoor planting with a recycling twist

## What you need:

- Plastic bottles (washed and dried)
- Scissors
- String
- Soil
- Plants: either grow them from seed or plant young plants. Mint, thyme, basil and rosemary are good starter herbs.

## What to do:

1. Cut around the lid of each plastic bottle to create a large opening, but make sure to leave the handle intact.
2. Invite the children to fill the bottles with soil and then plant the plants or seeds.
3. Thread the string through the handle and hang each bottle in a permanent position with plenty of light.
4. As there is no drainage, be careful not to overwater the plants.

## Top tip

Use a misting bottle to water the plants every few days instead of a watering can. Using a watering can may cause the water to pool in the bottom of the bottle.

### What's in it for the children?

This is a space-saving alternative to potting plants that will allow children to watch and investigate how plants grow. As most milk bottles are semi-transparent, children can watch the plants' root systems develop. They can also see when the soil is dry and needs watering, or if too much water has been added.

### Taking it forward

- Experiment with the types of plants you grow and invite the children to guess which will grow the quickest or tallest.

# Self-watering planters
## Use less water for your plants

## What you need:

- Plastic bottles (washed and dried)
- Scissors
- A sharp knife
- Soil
- Herbs or any edible plant such as chard, spinach or lettuce: either grow them from seed or plant young plants

## What to do:

1. Ask the children to cut the bottles in half using scissors, with an adult's help.
2. Remove the lids and using the sharp knife, very carefully cut small holes in the lids. An adult should do this bit.
3. Put the lid back on and insert the top halves of the bottles lid-side down into the bottom halves.
4. Invite the children to fill the bottles with soil and plant the herbs or other edible plants.
5. Water the plants until the water drains through the bottle cap into the bottom of the planter. This will allow the roots to absorb the water more easily.
6. Wait until all of the water is completely absorbed before watering again.

**Top tip** ⭐

Search online for 'self-watering planters' to see many variations of this simple activity.

### What's in it for the children?

This is an easy way to show children the importance of reducing water wastage as well as helping our indoor plants grow.

### Taking it forward

- Introduce some early scientific concepts to this activity by explaining evaporation and absorption to the children.

 **Health & Safety**

Risky play is an important element of Early Years education and that does include allowing children to use scissors when possible. An adult should help the children to ensure they are using the scissors safely.

# Plant drip feeders

Keep your plants watered

## What you need:

- Soda bottles (washed and dried)
- Scissors
- A sharp knife or a drill with a small drill piece
- Hanging baskets: established ones which have been filled with plants or new ones

## Top tip

Make sure the bottle is completely drained and that the soil is dry before inviting children to refill the drip feeder.

## What to do:

1. Ensure the outside of the bottles have the labels removed and there is no residue left in them.

2. Using the sharp knife or drill, cut 10 – 15 holes around the bottle at various heights. An adult should do this part.

3. Carefully cut off the base of the bottle (around 2 cm from the bottom) and keep the lid on the bottle. An adult should do this part too.

4. If you are starting a new hanging basket, add soil to the bottom of the basket, then place the water bottle with the bottle lid down into the middle and fill the basket with more soil, making sure the open end of the bottle is still exposed. Then plant your choice of plants.

5. If you are creating a drip feeder for an established plant pot, simply follow steps 1– 3 above and then add the bottle by digging a small hole in the middle of the plants.

6. Fill the bottle with water, which will slowly drip-feed the plants.

### What's in it for the children?

This activity teaches children that we need to respect and care for all living things for which we have responsibility.

### Taking it forward

- Use this method in outdoor garden beds with bigger bottles.

- To release water more slowly, only drill the holes on one side of the bottle and lay it down sideways on top of the soil.

✚ **Health & Safety**

Using a sharp knife on bottles can easily cause an injury from slipping. Make sure you have someone there to help you and take your time. Always keep the knife out of reach of children.

# Egg carton planter
Start your own garden

## What you need:
- A clean egg carton
- Soil
- Seeds
- Marker pens

## Top tip ⭐
You can buy seeds from shops or you can pick and dry seeds from fruits or vegetables you already have (tomatoes work well).

## What to do:
1. Ensure there is no residue on the egg carton and that it is intact with no holes anywhere.
2. Open and place the carton on a flat surface and help the children fill the holes where the eggs would normally be with soil.
3. Show the children how to plant a seed in one of the holes.
4. Encourage them to draw a picture to indicate which seeds went where on the lid of the carton.
5. Repeat until all of the egg holes are filled.
6. Lightly mist the soil, ensuring you don't overwater it as the egg carton will fall apart.
7. Place on a sunny windowsill to watch the seeds grow.
8. Water when the soil becomes dry. Once the seedlings reach maturity, cut around the individual soil spaces and plant them directly outdoors.

### What's in it for the children?
This easy and practical activity inspires a love of gardening in children as they plant their own seeds and watch them grow.

### Taking it forward
- Start a chart next to the growing carton. Children can estimate which seeds will grow the quickest, tallest, widest, and so on.

### ✚ Health & Safety
Ensure that egg cartons are completely clean before using them.

# Plant pot scarecrow

A recycled way to protect plants

## What you need:

- Recycled plastic plant pots with holes in the bottom – eight small, nine medium and two large (optional: an extra pot for the scarecrow's hat)
- Scissors
- Thick twine
- A large stick, such as a walking stick or broom handle

## What to do:

1. Invite the children to lay out the shape of the scarecrow in the following order: four small pots for each arm; four medium pots for each leg; two large pots for the body; one medium pot for the head.

2. Make each limb separately by threading the twine through the relevant pots, ensuring they are all facing the same way and are loosely spaced rather than tightly stacked together. Tie a knot at each end to secure each limb, leaving 10 cm of twine free at the end which will join the body.

3. To attach each limb to the body, thread the loose 10 cm of twine through the appropriate hole in the large body pots, then tie a knot on the inside of the body pots to secure it.

4. To make the body, the two large pots should be upside down on top of each other using the twine to connect the pots.

5. Place the head on top and attach it to the body and the stick using the twine. Then it's ready to be placed next to any outdoor plants.

### What's in it for the children?

Threading twine will help children develop their concentration and fine motor skills. This activity will create a fun scarecrow friend for children, which could be used as a stimulus for music and poetry.

### Taking it forward

- Experiment with different sizes of pots to create a family of scarecrows.
- Children could adapt the design to make animals to act as pets for the scarecrows.

## Top tip ⭐

Using terracotta pots will make the scarecrow last a lifetime. Look for ones with holes in them to avoid needing to drill holes in them.

# Newspaper plant pots

## Create biodegradable plant pots

## What you need:

- Old newspapers
- A large bowl
- Water
- A muffin tray or small cups
- Soil
- Seeds

## Top tip

Pansies, marigolds, nasturtiums and sweet peas are quite easy to grow from seed. Water sparingly while the plant is in a newspaper pot as overwatering will cause the pot to break down.

## What's in it for the children?

This is a practical and engaging way for children to grow their own plants in recycled pots. It is a good chance for children to manipulate materials with their hands: squeezing, stirring, ripping and shaping.

## Taking it forward

- Once the seedlings are around 15 cm tall, plant the whole pot in the garden. The newspaper will break down in the soil.

## What to do:

1. Invite the children to rip up the newspaper into long strips and place them in the bowl, one piece at a time.

2. Pour enough water into the bowl to cover all of the newspaper and ask the children to stir it with their hands.

3. Encourage the children to continue stirring and ripping the paper into smaller pieces. Once the newspaper resembles a mush, it is ready.

4. Invite the children to take a small handful of the paper mush and squeeze out some of the excess water.

5. Shape the mush to fit into each section of the muffin tray or in each of the cups, leaving space in the centre for soil.

6. Let the mush air-dry for several days and then place soil and seeds into the pre-made pots.

# Bird feeder balls

## Invite birds into your outdoor space

## What you need:

- Four tablespoons of coconut oil
- A microwave
- Two cups of bird seed mixture
- A muffin tin or ice cube tray
- A microwave-safe mixing bowl
- A wooden spoon
- String

## What to do:

1. Help the children measure the coconut oil into the microwave-safe bowl.

2. Microwave the oil for 30 – 45 seconds until it is melted. An adult should remove the oil from the microwave, being careful of the hot bowl and oil.

3. With adult help, the children can be invited to carefully add the bird seed and mix it so that it is entirely coated in the oil.

4. Divide the bird seed mixture into the muffin tin or ice cube tray.

5. Carefully push the end of the string into the top of the seed mixture, making sure it is covered. An adult should do this if the mixture is still hot.

6. Leave the mixture to harden completely for 24 hours in a cool place.

7. Remove the seed balls from the tin or tray and hang them outdoors for the birds to enjoy.

### What's in it for the children?

This is an easy activity that children can help with. Children will love seeing which birds they attract and will enjoy watching them.

### Taking it forward

- Experiment with different types of bird seeds as they will attract different birds.

- Try different types of bird feeder, for example, made from bottles (see page 18).

- Identify and log the birds that come frequently, to create a bird visitor's book.

### ✚ Health & Safety

These bird feeders may also attract mice or rats so hang them high up and ensure any seed which drops to the ground is swept up. Ensure the seed mix is free of anything the children are allergic to.

### Top tip ⭐

If you don't have access to a microwave, you could use a stove top to melt the coconut oil (adults only).

# Seed bombs
## Start your own green space

## What you need:

- Old newspapers
- A large bowl
- Water
- Seeds

## What to do:

1. This uses a similar method to the newspaper plant pots idea (page 14). Start by helping the children rip up the newspaper into long, thin strips and place them in the bowl.

2. Pour enough water into the bowl to cover all the newspaper and invite the children to stir it with their hands.

3. Encourage the children to rip the paper into smaller pieces as they stir. Once the newspaper resembles a mush, it is ready.

4. Invite the children to use their hands to squeeze off as much of the water as possible.

5. Add half a cup of seeds for each five cups of mush.

6. Stir in the seeds evenly and then shape the mixture into small balls, the size of a golf ball.

7. Let the mixture air-dry for 24 hours, then the balls are ready to be scattered. They could be scattered in any green space or hedgerow, or buried in plant pots.

## Top tip ⭐

The smaller the pieces of newspaper, the quicker the seed bomb will break down.

## What's in it for the children?

This is a different way of germinating seeds and can also be used to start conversations with children about plants and how they encourage wildlife. The outer layers protect the seeds from being eaten by birds or squirrels and provide a layer of compost to encourage seed growth. Children will also develop gross motor skills and large muscle development when they throw the seed bombs.

## Taking it forward

- Use different moulds or ice cube trays to create different shapes for the seed bombs.

- Seed bombs make great presents for family members or local communities.

- Children could focus on growing one type of plant and see which animals it attracts, for example, bees.

# Recycled bottle bird feeders

Another way to welcome feathered friends

## What you need:

- A large plastic bottle (washed and dried)
- A marker pen
- Chopsticks
- Scissors
- Masking tape
- Bird seed mix
- Twine or string

## What to do:

1. Place the bottle on a flat surface and help the children mark out the 'windows' for the birds to eat through. You don't need to do all the sides. The windows should be drawn halfway up the bottle.

2. Carefully cut out the windows using a pair of sharp scissors. An adult should do this bit.

3. Cut a small hole under each window, the same width as the chopsticks. Make sure there is also a hole at the same level on the opposite side. An adult should do this bit too.

4. Invite the children to thread the chopsticks through the holes on opposite sides until they are connected.

5. Cut a small hole in the lid of the bottle and use the twine to hang it outside.

6. Place the bird seed mixture in the bottle and see which birds land on the bird feeder.

### What's in it for the children?

This is an engaging way to teach children about respecting nature and will allow your setting's outdoor space to become a home for different species of birds.

### Taking it forward

- Start a bird watching book and ask children to identify and draw the different birds that are attracted to the outdoor space. Keep a bird watcher guide and binoculars to hand.

- Different birds will be attracted to different seeds, so try a variety.

 **Health & Safety**

Ensure the seed mix is free of anything the children are allergic to, such as nuts.

# Tyre flower beds

## Brighten up outdoor spaces

## What you need:

- An old tyre (these can be sourced from garages)
- A large hessian bag/burlap sack as wide as the tyre (these can be sourced at hardware stores or pet stores)
- Soil
- Plants: either seeds or young plants
- Scissors

## What to do:

1. Wash the old tyre with warm soapy water and let it dry.
2. Help the children to cut a medium-sized hole in the middle of one side of the hessian bag or burlap sack.
3. Place the sack over the tyre so that the hole exposes the middle of the tyre.
4. Ensure the tyre is in the position you want it to be in as a flowerbed, as it will become very heavy after it is filled with soil.
5. Invite the children to fill the tyre with soil and then plant flowers, vegetables or plants.

## Top tip

You could create a tyre chair using an old sack. Place the tyre inside the bag, sew the opening together, tuck the bag tightly under the tyre and place a cushion on top.

### What's in it for the children?

This idea will spark conversations with children around recycling, things that are difficult to recycle and how it is better to reuse or upcycle materials rather than throw them away.

### Taking it forward

- If you're creating a flower bed, stack multiple tyres in different levels to allow for more outdoor space. Alternatively, place tyres directly on top of each other to allow for larger plants or root vegetables to be grown.

# Regrowing vegetables

Teach children about reuse

## What you need:

- Vegetable ends: save the ends of celery, lettuce, pak choi, spring onions, etc.
- Small containers
- Water
- A windowsill

## Top tip

Other vegetables that can be replanted are potatoes and sweet potatoes that have sprouted (simply plant them in the garden and they will continue growing), garlic, cabbages, fennel, lemongrass and even the tops of carrots and pineapples.

## What to do:

1. Together with the children, wash all of the ends of the vegetables you are going to use.

2. Place the small containers on a windowsill with plenty of direct sunlight.

3. Place individual vegetable ends in the containers and fill them with enough water to cover the base. This is where the roots will begin growing.

4. Once the roots are established, show the children how to replant them in an outdoor space. Encourage the children to guess the rate at which they will grow and how tall each one will grow.

## What's in it for the children?

This activity shows children how to be resourceful by reusing food that would otherwise be thrown out. It also teaches children how vegetables are grown.

## Taking it forward

- Do some research and look into what other fruits and vegetables can be grown from cuttings or ends that would otherwise be thrown away.

- Talk to children about composting. See page 7 for a composting activity to try.

# Tyre bug hotel

Create a recycled oasis for minibeasts

## What you need:

- A tyre
- Natural materials: pinecones, sticks, leaves, bamboo pieces, etc.
- Pieces of measured and cut hardwood (the size depends on the tyre)
- Two large rocks

## Top tip

Recycled tyres can be found at local rubbish tips and recycling centres, or you could even ask a mechanic for an old tyre.

### What's in it for the children?

The amazing world of minibeasts teaches children about the environment around us and how we need to work to keep ecosystems healthy.

### Taking it forward

- Why not encourage the children to learn more about minibeasts? Use a container to carefully observe minibeasts moving before releasing them back to where they came from.

- Investigate the minibeasts at a closer distance with the children by making a bug-hunting kit. See page 24.

## What to do:

1. Place the tyre upright against a wall, in between the two large rocks for balance. It is usually best to place the tyre against a wall that doesn't receive direct sunlight.

2. Start at the bottom of the tyre and help the children put down one layer of the natural materials. Sticks are usually the best to start with as they provide a firm foundation for the next layers.

3. Once you are happy with the first layer, add one of the measured and cut pieces of hardwood. Try to wedge it into the inner lining of the tyre so that it is sturdy enough to hold the next layer.

4. Repeat step 2 with a different material. Remember that different insects and bugs will prefer different materials so the more variety on offer, the wider the range of minibeasts you can welcome into the outdoor space.

5. Repeat these steps until you've used all the pieces of wood and natural materials.

# Talking about worms

## Watch worms eating food scraps

## What you need:

- A large plastic bucket with a lid if possible
- A drill with a large drill piece
- A shovel
- Somewhere to store excess food scraps
- Newspaper
- Water

## Top tip

Never put cooked food, citrus, meat or dairy products into a wormery as they can harm worms. They can also start fermenting and attract rats.

### What's in it for the children?

Children will learn about worms and how they carry decaying material into the soil, where it is broken down into nutrients to help plants to grow. This activity will give children a better understanding of what we can do with food waste.

### Taking it forward

- You can build an indoor wormery with a glass jar, kept in a dark place. Watch the worms devour the food scraps from the outside.

### ✚ Health & Safety

Ensure that the drill is never left unattended and is always kept out of reach of children. Children should keep a safe distance while you are using the drill.

## What to do:

1. Place the bucket on a sturdy surface that will allow you to drill safely into it.

2. Drill three large holes into the bottom of the bucket and six to seven holes around the outside of the bucket. This will allow the worms to come and go as they please.

3. Dig a large hole in an outdoor space that doesn't receive direct sunlight.

4. Place the bucket in the hole, leaving the top 15 – 20 cm of the bucket above soil level. Fill the bucket with soil.

5. When you are ready, take the food scraps and place them inside the bucket on top of the soil. Place wet newspaper on top and water generously.

6. The worms will make their way through the holes in the bucket and they will recognise this as a good food source, filling the bucket with nutrient-rich worm castings.

# DIY bug-hunting kit
## Investigate minibeasts

## What you need:

- Two toilet roll tubes
- Masking tape
- Paints and paintbrushes
- String
- Scissors
- A jar or pot
- A small piece of gauze
- A rubber band

## What to do:

1. To make 'binoculars' for the bug-hunting kit, help the children secure the two toilet roll tubes together using masking tape.

2. Paint the binoculars and let them dry before cutting a small hole on either side of the tubes. An adult may need to help with this.

3. Thread a piece of string through the holes in the tubes and tie a knot at each end to create a strap for the binoculars.

4. Invite the children to prepare the jar or pot by collecting soil, grass and leaves and placing them inside the jar.

5. Encourage the children to go and find some minibeasts in the outside area. They can use their hands to carefully pick up insects or rest the jar next to an insect for it to crawl inside.

6. Show the children how to secure the top of the jar with gauze and a rubber band, so that they can observe the minibeasts for a while, before releasing the insects back into their habitat where they found them.

### What's in it for the children?
This activity allows children to look at and learn about bugs that live in gardens or local parks.

### Taking it forward

- Invite children to keep a journal of all of the minibeasts that are found. They could draw a picture of the bugs and use descriptive words to explain what they have drawn. This will allow them to recall facts more easily if they find the same bug again.

# CD sun catchers
## Catch the sun's reflections

## What you need:

- **Old CDs** (ideally with no labels on them)
- **String or twine**
- **Glue or acrylic paints** (optional)

## Top tip ⭐

You could use glue to stick two CDs together (shiny sides facing out) before threading them onto the sun catcher. Children could also paint the CDs (acrylic paints usually stick the best).

## What's in it for the children?

This is an interesting way to teach children about the sun and how light is reflected. For example, encourage the children to look at how the sun changes position in the sky over the course of the day.

## Taking it forward

- Adding different textures to the CDs will give different reflections. Why not try gemstones, coloured cellophane or different marker pen decorations?

## What to do:

1. Remove any plastic, stickers or residue that may be on the CDs.

2. Invite the children to line up a row of CDs on a flat surface, leaving a gap of 20 – 30 cm between each one.

3. Cut one long length of string or twine and lay it across all the CDs. This will become the main piece of string that all the CDs are attached to at the end.

4. Cut individual pieces of string for each CD and invite the children to thread a piece of string through each CD. An adult may need to help tie a knot to make a loop of string for each CD.

5. Each CD on a loop of string can then be threaded onto the main piece of string. The finished sun catcher can be hung up in an outdoor space, for example, between two branches of a tree or over a doorway.

# Tin can lanterns
Introduce children to tools

## What you need:

- Empty tin cans (washed and dried)
- Electrical tape
- Pipe cleaners
- A hammer
- A nail
- Battery-operated LED candles

## What to do:

1. Place a strip of electrical tape on the top of each tin can, covering any sharp edges and sealing them firmly.

2. Place the tin can on its side and hammer two holes at the top of the can on opposite sides. An adult should do this bit.

3. Help the children thread the pipe cleaner through on one side and twist. Place the other end in the opposite hole and twist again to create a handle.

4. Place the tin can on its side. Puncture holes around the can to let the light out. You could even try a pattern. An adult should do this bit.

5. Turn on the LED candle and place it in the tin can.

### Top tip ⭐

Watching adults use tools can inspire children to have a go with them (with supervision).

### What's in it for the children?

This is a fantastic activity to teach children about tool safety, as they are watching an adult use tools. The children will end up with a lantern they will be proud of.

### Taking it forward

- The lanterns can be placed around a mat and the children can lay down in between them for mindfulness activities.

- Showing children the hammer and nails could be a starting point for regular woodwork sessions. The girl in the photo is practising using a hammer on an offcut of wood (with supervision).

### ➕ Health & Safety

Children should not handle the tin cans before you have covered up the sharp edges with tape. Be aware that after time the tape may lose its stickiness and fall off.

# Glow-in-the-dark fun
## Turn a jar into a lamp

## What you need:

- Different-sized glass jars and their lids (washed and dried)
- Glow-in-the-dark paint: available from hardware stores (also called 'phosphorescent paint')
- A paintbrush
- String (optional)

## What to do:

1. Using a paintbrush, help the children paint the insides of the jars with the glow-in-the-dark paint. Alternatively, you can pour some of the paint into the jar, place the lid back on and ask the children to shake the jars to coat the inside.

2. Let the jars dry completely and place them in direct sunlight to absorb the light energy.

3. When it's dark they will glow. To make the jar into a lamp, tie some string around the top of the jar to create a handle.

4. These glow-in-the-dark jars could be used to create atmospheric storytelling sessions under canvas or blankets (indoors or outside).

### What's in it for the children?

This is an opportunity to create easy and practical homemade night lights for children and can help children who don't like the dark. It is a great way to use up old baby food jars.

### Taking it forward

- These are a great resource to take with you anytime you are outside and it's dark. You could also use them indoors with the lights off.
- Teach the children about why the jars need to be placed in the sunlight to 'charge' during the day.
- Children could take a lamp home with them and use it to do a 'magic hunt' with their parents or carers.

### Health & Safety

Ensure the glass jars are placed at an appropriate height so children can see them but not touch them. Children will naturally be inquisitive of the jars so may try to pull them down.

# Tin can wind chimes

## Make music with empty cans

## What you need:

- Empty tin cans of various sizes (washed and dried)
- Tape
- Paints and paintbrushes
- A hammer
- Nails
- String
- Small sticks

### What's in it for the children?

This is a fun musical activity that allows children to connect with nature and explore the lovely different sounds the wind makes.

### Taking it forward

- Help the children practise their listening skills by adding different recycled items, such as metal spoons or sticks, into the wind chimes to create different sounds.
- Hammer in more holes to some of the tins to change the sound.

### ✚ Health & Safety

Children should not handle the tin cans before you have covered up the sharp edges with tape. Be aware that after time the tape may lose its stickiness and fall off.

## What to do:

1. An adult should do steps 1 and 2. Place strips of tape around the open ends of the cans to cover up any sharp edges.

2. Hammer a nail into the bottom of each can to make a small hole. The hole should be big enough for the string to pass through.

3. Invite the children to paint the outside of the cans in different colours.

4. Help the children pass the string through the hole in the bottom of the can and tie a small stick at the bottom end of the string. This will help secure the string in place.

5. Tie all the tins together and hang them up high.

6. Wait for a nice breeze.

# Plastic bottle wind spirals

## Repurpose old bottles

## What you need:

- An assortment of different-sized plastic bottles (washed and dried)
- Scissors
- Paints and paintbrushes
- Some form of weight, e.g. a rock
- String

### What's in it for the children?

This simple activity will show children how sunlight reflects off different colours. When the wind is blowing quietly, the children will be able to hear the sound of the wind blowing through the spirals and watch the spirals 'dancing' in the wind.

### Taking it forward

- Instead of doing an even, continuous cut, why not experiment and cut different shapes and widths to make different spirals?
- Add natural items such as leaves to the finishing stages to add an extra decorative touch.

## What to do:

1. Invite the children to paint the outside of the different bottles and let them dry completely in the sun.
2. Using scissors, carefully poke a hole near the bottom of the bottle. Using the hole as a starting point, cut in one even, continuous line around the bottle, slowly sloping upwards to create the spiral.
3. Cut all the way to the top, leaving the bottle opening intact.
4. Thread the string through the opening and hang the bottle from a high position.
5. Gently pull the bottom of the spiral down and place a weight, such as a rock, in one of the grooves to extend the spiral downwards.
6. Ask the children where they would like to hang their wind spiral outside.

# Milk bottle windsocks

Explore weather changes

## What you need:

- Empty milk bottles (washed and dried)
- Scissors
- A hole punch
- Ribbon offcuts (ask your local florist if you can have any of their discarded ribbon)

## Top tip ⭐

Milk bottle lids can be saved and used to make finger puppets: see page 59. Also, when you cut the bottoms off the milk bottles, you can save these pieces to use as a paint tray in another activity.

### What's in it for the children?

This is a hands-on way to introduce children to the weather and can be used to discuss wind, cloud formation, the water cycle, and so on. The children also develop their fine motor skills by threading the ribbon through the holes.

### Taking it forward

- Use this activity as a base to look at changing weather patterns and begin identifying the different types of clouds.

- This is an excellent opportunity to expand children's vocabulary, for example, cumulonimbus clouds are associated with rain and thunderstorms.

## What to do:

1. Remove the lids and keep them for later.

2. Carefully cut the bottoms off the milk bottles (around 5 cm from the base). An adult may need to do this bit.

3. Help the children to use the hole punch to cut as many holes as possible around the bases of the milk bottles.

4. Invite the children to thread ribbons through the holes and tie knots at the top, leaving as much of the ribbon free flowing as possible.

5. Go outside and hold the windsocks up to see which way the wind is blowing by seeing which direction the ribbons blow.

# Homemade bubble blowers

## An outdoor activity reusing bottles

## What you need:

- Plastic bottles (washed and dried)
- Washing-up liquid
- Scissors
- Water
- A small flat container

## Top tip ⭐

After using the bubble blowers, wash them with warm soapy water and leave them to dry ready for next time.

### What's in it for the children?

Children can have fun blowing their own bubbles. They can experiment with air flow, for example, by blowing softly to make smaller bubbles, or blowing very slowly to create different sizes of bubble.

### Taking it forward

- Add a few drops of an essential oil (lavender, lemongrass, etc.) to the bubble mixture to bring sensory delight to the activity when the bubbles pop.

### ➕ Health & Safety

Make the children aware of the dangers of inhaling the washing-up liquid mixture. Ensure they breathe in well away from the bottle top, before blowing out through it.

## What to do:

1. There are two methods to create these bubble blowers. For both methods, make a bubble mixture by stirring together 1/4 cup of water and one tablespoon of washing-up liquid.

2. For the first method, you will need to cut off the bottom of the plastic bottle (3 – 4 cm from the base).

3. Dip the cut end into the bubble mixture and invite the children to blow through the bottle top to create their own bubbles.

4. The second method is simpler. Just take the lid off the bottle and make the bubble mixture in the bottle. Squeeze the bottle quickly to create bubbles.

# Water xylophone

Experiment with water and sound

## What you need:

- Six or seven glass jars or bottles of the same size (washed and dried)
- Water
- Food colouring
- A stick

## What to do:

1. Line up the jars in a row and place a few drops of different food colouring into each jar. Ensure the colours do not mix accidentally.

2. Fill each glass jar with a different quantity of water. You could make the differences very big (increase by 50 ml at a time) or very small (increase by 10 ml at a time).

3. Encourage the children to tap the rim of each glass jar with a stick and listen to the different musical notes.

4. The children can experiment with making their own music.

## Top tip ⭐

Food colouring is harmless to plants, so once you've finished the activity, tip the water onto any thirsty plants.

### What's in it for the children?

This activity introduces a science concept that interests children while also allowing them to conduct auditory experiments with different sounds and timbres. The jars will introduce them to the concept of different notes, while changing how they tap the glass will create different sounds.

### Taking it forward

- There are many songs that children can recreate using three to five notes. 'Hot Cross Buns' is a great example as it only has three notes. Create a system of notating the sounds into a simple tune for the children to learn.

# Recycled boats

Will it or won't it float?

## What you need:

- An assortment of recycled items, such as cardboard boxes, glass jar lids, bottle tops, etc.
- Sticky tack
- Straws or lollipop sticks
- Paper, cut into triangles
- Glue
- A large bucket of water
- A notebook, to be used as a ship's log

## What to do:

1. Start by making ships' sails. Help the children fold the paper triangles in half and glue them to the top of their chosen masts (lollipop sticks or straws).

2. Collect recycled items to be the boat bases. The children can create their own options.

3. Using sticky tack, attach the masts to the middle of the boats.

4. Ask the children to estimate how long they think the boats will float and record this in the ship's log (a notebook).

5. Place the boats in the bucket of water to see if they sink or float. If the sail touches the water, this would be deemed as sinking.

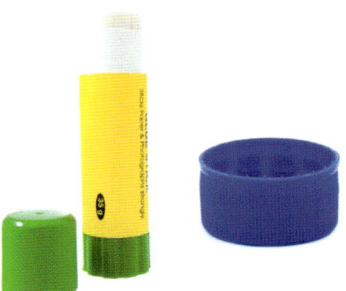

### What's in it for the children?

A single bottle top, despite being very small, will still make a great boat. Children can then experiment with what would be needed to make a bigger boat. This activity also introduces children to different scientific concepts: floating and sinking, balance, exploration, estimating and observing.

### Taking it forward

- Add weights such as stones to the boats that float to test them further. Choose similarly sized stones and estimate which boat will be able to handle the added load.

### Top tip ⭐

Add sticky tack to the bottom of the boats to give them a bit more weight, so that they don't capsize straight away!

# Water channels

Create plastic bottle waterfalls

## What you need:

- Different-sized plastic bottles (washed and dried)
- A wall or a large piece of wood
- Electrical tape
- Scissors
- A container
- Water

## What to do:

1. Take all the lids off the bottles. Carefully cut a hole in the side of each bottle towards the bottom. An adult should do this bit.

2. Ask the children to arrange and hold the bottles against the wall or piece of wood, starting from the top and working down. The bottles should be facing down at an angle to allow water to flow from one bottle to the next, with the lid of each bottle positioned so that the water will fall into the hole in the one below.

3. Secure the bottles with electrical tape, ensuring that the openings (the tops of the bottles and holes in the bases) are not covered.

4. Continue securing the bottles down the wall or piece of wood until you reach the bottom.

5. Place a container at the bottom to collect the water so it can be reused.

6. Invite the children to pour water in the top bottle and watch it run down the channel.

### What's in it for the children?

There are a multitude of learning outcomes within this activity: estimating time, learning about water flow, counting… But one of the main things is that it is fun and will keep children playing and engaged for extended periods of time.

### Taking it forward

- Create multiple channels for the water to flow through.

- Add food colouring to the water to create a race in order to compare how quickly the water flows through each channel. Children can estimate outcomes and record the results.

# Ice bowling

Great for cooling down in summer

## What you need:

- Ten clear plastic bottles (washed and dried)
- Water
- Food colouring
- A balloon
- A freezer
- Scissors

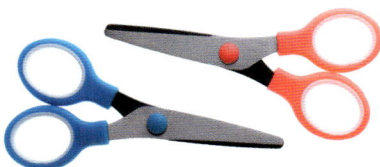

## What to do:

1. Remove the labels from the bottles and fill them with water.

2. Place a few drops of food colouring into each bottle and screw the lids back on.

3. Carefully place a few drops of food colouring into each balloon.

4. Fill the balloons with water and tie off the ends. Give them a shake to make sure the food colouring is mixed.

5. Place the balloons in the freezer for 24 – 48 hours until they are frozen solid.

6. Place the coloured bottles in a triangular ten-pin bowling formation.

7. Take the ice balloons from the freezer and cut off the knotted ends. Invite the children to use them as bowling balls to knock down the homemade bowling pins.

### What's in it for the children?

This activity will develop children's gross motor skills as well as contribute towards large muscle development, all while keeping them cool in summer.

### Taking it forward

- Use the bowling set to help with subtraction. For example, you could ask, 'We started with ten bottles and you knocked four down. How many are left standing?'

# Bottle turtles

Recycle bottles for water play

## What you need:

- A clear plastic bottle or plastic cup (washed and dried)
- Scissors
- Some foam or a sponge
- A glue gun
- Googly eyes with sticky backs
- Marker pens
- A container of water

### What's in it for the children?

These bottle turtles are a fun addition to water play and, if you make several, they are a great resource to put out during role play or small world play.

### Taking it forward

- Use the turtles to talk about scientific concepts such as floating and sinking.
- There are many fun songs you can sing with the turtles. Look online for the lyrics to 'I Had a Little Turtle'.

### ✚ Health & Safety

Never touch the hot end of a glue gun. Glue guns should be used with adult supervision.

## What to do:

1. Start by cutting the base off the bottle or cup (around 5 cm from the bottom). An adult should do this bit. This will act as the turtle shell.
2. Place this on top of the foam or sponge to get an idea of the shape of the turtle.
3. Help the children draw the outline of the turtle's head, flippers and tail on the foam or sponge using a marker pen.
4. Carefully cut around the outline. An adult may need to do this bit.
5. Use the glue gun to connect the foam or sponge to the shell. An adult will need to do this.
6. Using marker pens, encourage the children to draw a design on the turtle's shell. Attach the googly eyes to the head.
7. Place the turtle into the water and you will have a floating turtle toy.

# Tissue box animal feet

Great for animal role play

## What you need:

- Tissue boxes, two per child
- PVA glue
- Colourful tissue paper or paint
- Cardboard
- Scissors
- Paint
- String (optional)

## What to do:

1. Invite the children to decorate their tissue boxes using PVA glue and coloured tissue paper. They could also use paint instead of tissue paper. Once dry, the PVA glue will make the tissue boxes tougher.

2. Cut triangles out of cardboard and encourage the children to stick them to the front of their tissue boxes to represent toes. The children can use as many toes as they like and experiment with shapes and sizes.

3. Let the tissue boxes dry completely and then invite the children to place their feet in the openings.

4. If the opening is too big for little feet, cut two holes in the bottom of the box and thread string through. Tie knots at both ends of the string to create a strap.

5. The children can enjoy stomping around with their new animal feet!

### What's in it for the children?

This fun activity allows children to create their own imaginative worlds, for example, stomping around the room as dinosaurs or pretending to be tigers prowling in the jungle. Nurseries often go through a lot of tissues: this is a good way to reuse the boxes!

### Taking it forward

- Use different colours and patterns to represent different animals.
- Create a whole set of animal feet for role play scenarios.

# Egg carton sorters
## A fun maths activity

## What you need:

- Empty egg cartons
- Scissors
- Paints and paintbrushes
- Items to be sorted: buttons, marbles, LEGO™ pieces, etc. If you are doing this activity outside, ensure there are items such as leaves, flowers or seeds.

## Top tip

If you are using the cartons for addition and subtraction, it may help to draw or add an addition or subtraction symbol in the middle of the egg carton.

## What to do:

1. Cut and divide the egg cartons into different denominations, such as twos, threes or fours, or leave the cartons whole.

2. Invite the children to paint the egg cartons a colour of their choice.

3. Once the egg cartons are dry, use them to teach the children colour recognition and matching. You could ask, 'Can you find and place green objects from around the room in the green container?' or 'Can you fill the egg carton with four different objects?'.

4. You can also teach basic mathematical skills such as addition and subtraction. For example, you could ask, 'If there is one item in this section and I add one more item, what does it equal?'

5. Take the egg carton sorters outside, if you can, so that the children can sort natural items by colour.

## What's in it for the children?

This is a fun way for children to develop their fine motor skills and learn early mathematical concepts: sorting, matching, counting, addition and subtraction.

## Taking it forward

- Paint the individual sections of the egg cartons different colours to extend the colour recognition element of this activity.

- Practise fine motor skills by giving the children pegs or tweezers to use instead of picking the items up with their hands.

 **Health & Safety**

Be aware that children with egg allergies can react to egg cartons that may have traces of eggs on them, so ensure the cartons are completely clean.

# DIY puzzles
Repurpose old pictures

## What you need:

- Old pictures (e.g. from magazines)
- Old cardboard (e.g. cereal boxes)
- Glue
- Scissors
- A marker pen

## Top tip ⭐

To make the puzzles last longer, you could laminate the pictures before the children cut them into puzzle pieces. However, this might make it harder for children to cut the pieces by themselves.

### What's in it for the children?

This is a practical and engaging way for children to create their own puzzles and learn matching skills as they reassemble them.

### Taking it forward

- Using a piece of cardboard, let the children paint or draw on it and create their own piece of art before turning it into a puzzle.
- Add numbers or letters to the individual puzzle pieces to improve children's number recognition skills.

## What to do:

1. Invite the children to choose a picture and help them glue it onto a piece of cardboard.

2. Using a marker pen, help the children draw a design on the back of the cardboard to represent the puzzle pieces. Try simple shapes to begin with and increase the difficulty depending on the age and stage of the children.

3. Carefully cut along the design to make the puzzle pieces.

4. Scatter the pieces and encourage the children to reassemble their handmade puzzles.

# Eco-bricks

Put non-recyclable plastic to good use

## What you need:

- Non-recyclable plastics: cling film, plastic lids, wrappers, bottle labels, etc.
- Large plastic bottles (washed and dried)
- Scissors
- A stick or wooden spoon (optional)

## Top tip

You could ask the children to collect non-recyclable plastics that have been used at home in the run-up to doing this activity.

### What's in it for the children?

This is a great ongoing activity for children that teaches them about how we make items that cannot be recycled useful for the community. It is also a great addition to your setting's construction area: eco-bricks can be used to create buildings, towers and castles.

### Taking it forward

- There is an app that can be downloaded for people who are looking for donations of eco-bricks that are then repurposed into greenhouses, chairs, work benches, and so on.

## What to do:

1. Place the bottles in a place that is easily accessible for the children.

2. Collect the non-recyclable plastic and cut it into strips or smaller pieces. An adult may need to do this bit.

3. Show the children how to push the strips and pieces of plastic into the bottles. You may need a stick or wooden spoon handle to push the pieces down.

4. Continue until the bottle is completely full and firm. You can keep adding to the bottles over weeks or months until they are full.

5. You now have eco-bricks ready to be part of a building plan or donated to a community project.

# Plastic bottle igloo

A great addition to role play

## What you need:

- As many plastic bottles as you can find (washed and dried)
- A marker pen
- A glue gun
- A large cardboard base

## Top tip ⭐

You could ask a local café or coffee shop to save their milk bottles for you.

### What's in it for the children?

Although a time-consuming activity, this is a great way to develop concentration and encourage children to persevere.

### Taking it forward

- Invite the children to use the igloos in role play activities.
- Use the igloo as a starting point for children to learn about igloos and how they are made. This can form the basis for some amazing conversations about Inuits and their igloo homes.

### ➕ Health & Safety

Never touch the hot end of a glue gun. Glue guns should be used with adult supervision.

## What to do:

1. Start with the cardboard base on the floor and draw a circle to mark the outline of the base of the igloo (the size of the circle will determine how many bottles are needed).

2. Using the glue gun, start by gluing the bottles end to end around the circle, leaving a gap for the door. An adult will need to do this bit and the children may be able to help.

3. Glue the next layer of bottles on top. Ensure this layer overhangs towards the centre of the igloo to create the dome effect. Each layer should use half of the number of bottles than the previous layer.

4. Repeat until you have reached the top.

5. Make the entrance by gluing the bottles on top of each other, lids facing outwards, in an arc shape. Glue the arc to the opening.

# Recycled marble run

A classic activity with a recycled twist

## What you need:

- Toilet roll or kitchen roll tubes
- Masking tape
- A backing for the marble run, e.g. a large piece of cardboard or sheet of wood
- Marbles
- Scissors
- A small container

## What to do:

1. Decide with the children where you want the marble run to be created, ensuring it is not anywhere that will be knocked over or need to be moved.
2. Tape the first cardboard tube horizontally against the backing, around one metre high.
3. Ask the children to place a marble in the starting tube and, experimenting with angles, decide where the marble should drop next.
4. Encourage the children to continue placing different-sized tubing downwards to create a 'run' for the marble to travel down.
5. Place a container at the bottom to collect the marbles.

### What's in it for the children?

Children love marble runs and this is an easy way to allow them to use their imagination designing and creating their own marble run out of recycled materials. This is a great introduction to scientific concepts such as speed and direction and can provide a chance to talk about gravity.

### Taking it forward

- Why not try introducing different designs to older children and allowing them to explore what happens? For example, a large drop means a faster marble that may be able to travel back up a connecting tube.

### Top tip ⭐

More ambitious marble runs can be created with cardboard (like the one in the photo) but toilet roll tubes connected in a line are all you really need!

# Newspaper structures

**Use old newspapers**

## What you need:

- Old newspapers
- Masking tape
- Scissors

## What to do:

1. Collect old newspapers and remove the staples (an adult should do this bit). Separate the pages and group two to three together.

2. Invite the children to roll the newspaper up tightly and place masking tape at the top, middle and bottom. Encourage them to create different sizes of rolls: long, short, wide, narrow, and so on.

3. Continue this process until the children have enough rolls to start building towers or other constructions, like frames.

4. The children can secure their constructions with masking tape to prevent the newspaper unfurling.

5. The children can let their imaginations run wild to create as many different types of towers or shapes as they can. They could even try and create a replica of a famous landmark, for example, Big Ben.

### What's in it for the children?

This is an easy and fun modelling activity that can be extended in many different ways. For example, it can be a great resource to support role play and storytelling.

### Taking it forward

- Once completed, the children could paint their structures.

- Encourage children to hypothesise and introduce mathematical concepts. For example, ask, 'Can your tower hold the weight of...?' or 'Do you think your tower is as tall as ...?'

# Egg carton building blocks

## A homemade construction resource

## What you need:

- Egg cartons, ideally seven to eight cartons
- Paints and paintbrushes
- Scissors

## What to do:

1. Start by looking over the egg cartons and ensuring there is no egg residue left on any of them.

2. Invite the children to paint all of the egg cartons (inside and out) with a variety of colours and leave them to dry.

3. Use scissors to cut up the egg cartons into different sizes: one section, rows of two, rows of five, etc. An adult may need to do this bit.

4. The children can use their new building blocks however they like.

### What's in it for the children?

This is a fun way for children to repurpose materials and create new resources that can be used in a multitude of different ways. They could create towers or castles, or use them for sums (for example, adding different sections together).

### Taking it forward

- Use this resource as an introduction to mathematical concepts, using the blocks to represent different values, for example, one block + one block = two blocks. Increase the number of blocks to make this more challenging.

 **Health & Safety**

Be aware that children with egg allergies can react to egg cartons that may have traces of eggs, so ensure the cartons are completely clean.

# Plastic bottle flowers

A recycled addition to your garden space

## What you need:

- Plastic bottles (washed and dried)
- A glue gun
- A stick
- Scissors
- Paints or marker pens
- Small rocks or dirt

## What to do:

1. An adult will need to do steps 1 – 4. First, remove all the labelling from the bottles and cut them in half. Put the bottom halves of the bottles to one side.

2. With the top halves, cut long lengths from the bottom up to the lid. Try to make at least eight cuts as they will represent the petals of a plastic bottle flower.

3. Push back all the plastic lengths until they remain flat on their own.

4. Using the glue gun, glue the inside of the bottle lids and attach them to the sticks. Leave them to dry.

5. Invite the children to place the small rocks or dirt in the bottom half of the bottle. This will be the plant pot.

6. The children can place the plastic flower on the stick firmly in the plant pot and decorate them however they choose.

> **Top tip** ⭐
>
> You could also hang the flowers on string as fun decorations.

### What's in it for the children?

This activity is a great way for using plastic bottles and teaches children about repurposing.

### Taking it forward

- Before attaching the stick to the bottle flowers, you could use the bottle flowers as paintbrushes to create an interesting painting. This is similar to the natural paintbrushes idea (page 52).

- Why not try and make a whole flower bed out of recycled flowers?

### ✚ Health & Safety

Glue guns must always be used by an adult. Never touch the end of the glue gun (the heating component).

# Toilet roll fireworks

Explore textures with paint

## What you need:

- Toilet or kitchen roll tubes
- Paints
- Paper
- Scissors

## What to do:

1. Make sure all the different tubes you are using have all of the paper removed from the outside.

2. Using scissors, help the children carefully cut short or long lengths from the bottom of the roll towards the middle. An adult may need to do this for young children.

3. Invite the children to carefully pull the cut lines out using their hands to make them flat.

4. Show the children how to dip the splayed ends in paint and press onto paper using whatever motion they choose: swirling or dragging, for example.

5. Cut differently sized lengths to create smaller or bigger fireworks.

## Top tip

You could use a similar technique to turn toilet rolls into octopuses instead of fireworks! Children could then decorate the octopuses instead of dipping them in paint. Remind the children to only make eight tentacles!

### What's in it for the children?

This activity allows children to develop their fine motor and hand-eye coordination skills in a fun and creative way. Using toilet and kitchen roll tubes means that children can experiment with different sizes.

### Taking it forward

- Experiment using the same method on different materials (such as milk bottles and paper) to test the principle of cause and effect. Discuss with children whether the outcome remains the same or if there is a reason this activity works best with cardboard dipped in paint.

# Repair broken crayons

## What can you do with broken crayons?

## What you need:

- Broken crayons
- Ovenproof moulds (these are usually made from silicon and are reusable)
- An oven
- Oven gloves

### What's in it for the children?

This is a great way to teach children about reusing items and not throwing things out just because they are broken.

### Taking it forward

- Introduce the children to scientific concepts, such as temperature, melting points and density.
- Discuss how and why things melt and which materials might not melt.

### ✚ Health & Safety

Only adults should use the oven and it should never be left unattended. Ensure that the moulds are completely cool before allowing children to handle them.

## What to do:

1. Ensure that none of the crayons have any paper or wrappers left on them.

2. Invite the children to break the crayons down further into smaller pieces as this will speed up the melting process.

3. Place the crayons in the ovenproof moulds. Make sure they are slightly overfilled as they will melt down.

4. Place in a preheated oven (200 degrees, or 180 degrees for fan ovens) for 10 to 15 minutes. Once the crayons are completely melted down, remove them from the oven using oven gloves, being careful as they will be hot. An adult should do this bit.

5. Let the melted crayons cool completely. Once solid, pop them out of the mould and the children will have brand-new crayons.

# Old pens become paint

## What can you do with dried-out pens?

## What you need:

- Old dried-out marker pens
- Water
- Bottles, one bottle for each colour of marker pen.

## What to do:

1. Help the children sort the dried-out marker pens by colour.
2. Place the marker pens (tip first with no lid) into the bottles by colour, so that you have, for example, one bottle of red markers, one bottle of blue markers, and so on.
3. Pour water into the bottles (the smaller the quantity of water, the more concentrated the colour will be).
4. Leave the bottles for 12 – 14 hours for the colours to mix with the water.
5. Once fully mixed, the coloured liquid can be used to spray paints onto paper or poured into containers and used as watercolours.

### What's in it for the children?

This is an easy way to show children how to reuse items that appear to be broken. The pens that have been dipped into water may also be (temporarily) brought back to life by this activity and could be used for mark making. Children can also develop their fine motor skills by using the trigger action of the spray bottles.

### Taking it forward

- Instead of only having one colour in each bottle, try mixing them. Before adding the water, let the children guess what colour they think will be created by different colour combinations.

# Natural paintbrushes

Create your own paintbrushes

## What you need:

- An outdoor space with sticks, leaves, moss, etc.
- Rubber bands
- Paper
- Paints

## What to do:

1. Invite the children to go on a scavenger hunt in the outdoor space, collecting sticks, leaves, moss, and so on. Clean off any excess dirt from the items.

2. Position the sticks on a table. These will form the paintbrush handles.

3. Ask the children to choose an object to form the bristles of their natural paintbrush. This could be leaves or moss, for example. Try experimenting with mixing different textures, and adding more or less of the materials.

4. Help the children place their objects at the end of the stick, and secure them with a rubber band.

5. The children can dip the 'bristles' into paint and start painting and printing onto paper.

## ✚ Health & Safety

Ensure that the outdoor area is free from any dangerous debris or plants.

## What's in it for the children?

By sourcing materials in outdoor spaces, children will gain a better understanding and respect for nature and realise that not everything needs to be bought.

## Taking it forward

● Invite children to do printing and rubbing with natural items. For rubbing, lay the different found objects from nature onto a table and place a piece of paper over the top. Using the side of a crayon, gently rub back and forth over the objects to reveal the different patterns found on each one.

# Natural paints

Make paint with food scraps

## What you need:

- Food scraps
- Pots
- A stove top
- Water
- A colander
- A container
- Paintbrushes
- Paper

## Top tip

Vivid-coloured food scraps work well, for example, kale, spinach, beetroot or berries. Make sure you use similar colours together, though.

## What to do:

1. Run the food scraps under water to wash off any excess dirt.

2. Place a pot of water on a stove and fill it with the scraps of similar colours. There should be enough water to cover them.

3. Bring the water to a boil and let the mixture simmer for one hour. This should be done by an adult.

4. Let the mixture cool completely.

5. Drain the scraps through a colander into a container to catch the coloured water.

6. Throw out the food scraps or put them in the compost – or if possible, you could use a blender to make them into stock for soup.

7. Invite the children to use paintbrushes, paper and the coloured water to create beautiful watercolour paintings.

## What's in it for the children?

By reusing old food scraps, we are teaching children to be less wasteful. Encouraging the children to guess what colours will come from each scrap adds a science element to the activity.

## Taking it forward

- Mix flour and water to make a paste, and then add pre-made natural paints to create a thicker texture of paint.

- Add different-coloured food scraps to the water to expose children to colour mixing and show them how some colours are created.

➕ **Health & Safety**

Be aware of any food allergies in the group before starting this activity. The stove should only be used by an adult and should never be left unattended.

# Bottle top stampers

**Make recycled stamps**

## What you need:

- Plastic bottle tops of assorted sizes
- Different types of string
- A glue gun
- Paints

## What to do:

1. Wash the bottle tops thoroughly and let them dry.
2. Cut the different lengths of string: up to 10 cm long.
3. Put some of the hot glue on the flat side of the bottle top. An adult should do this bit.
4. Arrange the string in flat patterns on top of the glue ensuring that all of the string is attached to the lid.
5. Once dry, use the bottle top stamps with paints for different stamping activities.

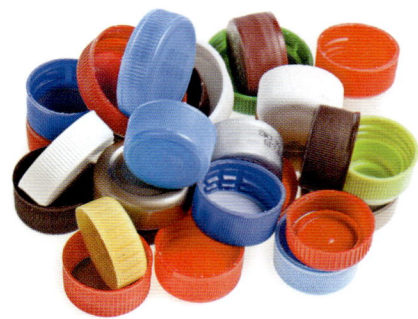

### What's in it for the children?

This is an easy way to use leftover bottle tops from milk or juice bottles for art activities. Children will develop their fine motor skills through grasping the bottle tops and practising their pincer grip.

### Taking it forward

- Extend the children's letter, number or shape recognition by using the string to represent different letters, numbers or symbols.
- Older children can use these stamps to create their names or basic words.

# Sock caterpillars

## Reuse old socks

## What you need:

- Clean long socks
- Rubber bands
- A marker pen
- Some form of stuffing (scrunched up newspaper works well)
- Pipe cleaners

## What to do:

1. Help the children scrunch the newspaper into lots of small balls.
2. Stuff the newspaper balls into the socks.
3. Using a rubber band, fasten the end of the socks.
4. Place additional rubber bands over each section of the socks to represent the different parts of a caterpillar's body.
5. Using the marker pen, draw eyes on the end section and decorate by drawing markings on the bodies.
6. Secure the pipe cleaner around the 'head' section of the caterpillars and twist to represent the antennae.

## Top tip ⭐

You don't just have to use socks! You could recycle any old clothing you have (jeans or long-sleeved shirts, for example,) and use the same method to create fun animals.

### What's in it for the children?

This is an easy way to show children how old clothes can be repurposed. The caterpillar socks can be incorporated into role play or storytelling.

### Taking it forward

- Socks don't just have to be caterpillars; they could be turned into other animals. For example, connect several newspaper-filled socks in a line to make a really long snake.

# Storytelling bottle lids

## Reuse damaged storybooks

## What you need:

- A damaged storybook that cannot be repaired, or photocopied pages from a favourite book or magazine
- PVA glue
- Plastic bottle lids
- Scissors
- Pens (optional)
- Lollipop sticks or toilet roll tubes (optional)

## Top tip

Ask children to bring in old family photos from home and stick them onto the bottle lids to add a more personalised touch to the story.

### What's in it for the children?

This activity is great to help children to recall their favourite stories or create their own versions using the lids as prompts for the sequence or characters.

### Taking it forward

- Children can use their knowledge of repurposing and recycling materials and make an entire story out of items that would have otherwise been thrown away. A story could be created featuring toilet roll trees, tissue box houses, and so on.

## What to do:

1. Let the children go through the storybook and find pictures of characters or objects that can be cut out to fit onto bottle lids.

2. Invite the children to cut carefully around their chosen objects or characters. If needed, use the bottle lids as a guide: place them over the picture, trace around the edge and then cut out.

3. Glue the individual pictures onto the bottle lids and let them dry.

4. Once dried, the lids can be used to retell the story. The children can use their memory of the story to place the lids in order or create their own stories.

5. The lids can be used on their own, or you could glue them onto lollipop sticks or toilet roll tubes to represent the characters as little puppet props.

# Snail finger puppets

## Create pipe cleaner puppets

## What you need:

- Different-coloured long pipe cleaners, one per child
- Googly eyes
- A milk bottle lid, one per child
- A glue gun
- Marker pens (optional)

## Top tip

If you are making finger puppets for children with bigger hands, simply start the finger puppet halfway up their fingers.

## What's in it for the children?

This is an easy and practical activity that can be used for telling stories and to extend children's vocabulary at the same time. Expose children to new descriptive words as you tell a story about a snail: 'astonishing', 'courteous', 'cheerful', 'delighted', 'ecstatic', and so on.

## Taking it forward

- Incorporate the snail finger puppets into songs and story times. Try 'The Snail Song':

  *Two little eyes, one and two*

  *One pretty shell, nice to meet you*

  *He has no legs, just a tail*

  *It's a snail, it's a snail, it's a snail.*

## ✚ Health & Safety

Glue guns can become very hot: always use under adult supervision and never touch the end of the gun.

## What to do:

1. Make a small circle at the very end of the pipe cleaner and twist it. This should fit around a child's finger but not too tightly.

2. Start wrapping the pipe cleaner around the base of the child's finger, ensuring it is not too tight and that it can slip off easily.

3. Bend the final 4 cm of the pipe cleaner into two horizontal edges.

4. Remove the pipe cleaner from the child's finger, and use a glue gun to stick the eyes onto the horizontal edges. An adult should do this bit.

5. Glue the bottle tops onto the top of the wrapped pipe cleaner to represent a snail's shell. The children could use marker pens to decorate the snail's shell further.

# Cardboard box guitars

## Make junk instruments

## What you need:

- A large, empty cereal box (or an empty tissue box with the opening intact)
- Scissors
- Large rubber bands
- A kitchen roll tube
- Glue
- Paint and paintbrushes (optional)

## What to do:

1. Start by cutting a large hole in the centre of one side of a cereal box, so that it looks like the hole in a tissue box. An adult may need to do this bit.

2. Carefully stretch and place the rubber bands over the opening of the cardboard box.

3. Using the glue, attach the kitchen roll tube to one end of the box to make the neck of the guitar.

4. Show the children how to pluck the rubber bands to make music!

### What's in it for the children?

This is a fun musical activity that allows children to be creative and use their imagination while also recycling cardboard. This could become a painting activity if you invite the children to paint the cereal boxes and kitchen role tubes before making the guitars.

### Taking it forward

- Make a whole range of instruments using recycled materials. Empty baby formula tins make great drums while old plastic bottles can be filled with small objects and transformed into maracas.

- Introduce different musical words to the children, such as 'beat', 'tap', 'chord', and 'strum'.

### ✚ Health & Safety

Test the rubber bands beforehand to make sure they are stretchy enough so they don't snap and cause injury. If you are extending this activity using formula tins, be aware that the inside rim of the tins can be extremely sharp. You could seal the rims with tape.

# Egg carton crocodiles

Egg cartons come alive

## What you need:

- Six or seven egg cartons
- A hole punch
- Scissors
- String
- Different-coloured paints and paintbrushes

## What to do:

1. Ensure the egg cartons are completely clean with no egg residue left on them.

2. Invite the children to paint all the egg cartons their chosen colour and leave them to dry completely.

3. Arrange the egg cartons as follows:

    One carton for the mouth

    Two for the body

    Two for the tail

    Half a carton for each of the four legs.

4. Help the children connect the parts by punching holes and trying them together with string. Make two to three holes at each connection point to ensure it is strong.

5. The children can let their imaginations run free with their very own pet crocodile!

### What's in it for the children?

This is a great role play and creative play activity. The crocodile makes a nice prop for singing songs as well, for example, 'Three Cheeky Monkeys'.

### Taking it forward

- Collect different containers (milk bottles, egg cartons, bottle tops) and give them to the children along with a selection of animal identification books. See what other animals could be created using loose parts.

### ✚ Health & Safety

Be aware that children with egg allergies can react to egg cartons that may have traces of eggs, so ensure the cartons are completely clean.

# Recycled music station

Repurpose old pots, pans and other kitchen items

## What you need:

- A variety of old pots, pans and other kitchen items such as sticks, spoons or ladles
- String
- Somewhere to hang the items from (outside is usually best)

## Top tip

Charity shops will usually have great selection of old pots, pans and other kitchen items of different shapes and sizes.

## What to do:

1. Lay out all of the pots, pans and utensils, having made sure they are all clean, dry and do not have any sharp edges on them.

2. Tie a piece of string to the handle of each item. Use different lengths of string so that the pots, pans and other kitchen items hang at different heights.

3. Hang the items up for the children to bang at different heights and angles. For example, you could hang them from a wall or an overhead structure.

4. Experiment with hitting them with different items: sticks, spoons, ladles, etc.

## What's in it for the children?

This activity allows children to create their own music and experiment with their dance and movement skills. They can use sticks, wooden spoons or ladles to make sounds with the pots, or they can use their hands.

## Taking it forward

● Play a simple song on the music station and invite the children to replicate it. 'Hot Cross Buns' is an easy song to learn as it only has three notes and children will pick up the rhythm quite quickly.

# Bottle top snakes

## Use up bottle lids

## What you need:

- Plastic bottle tops of various sizes
- String
- A hammer
- A nail
- Googly eyes
- Pipe cleaners, sticks or scrap paper (optional)

### What's in it for the children?

This is a great activity to develop children's cognitive skills and hand-eye coordination, and also practise fine motor skills.

### Taking it forward

- By adding additional holes to certain bottle tops and starting a new run of tops, the snake could be transformed into a number of other different animals.

### ✚ Health & Safety

Hammers should be used with adult supervision. Always take your time when using the hammer and make sure there are no distractions around so you are able to concentrate.

## What to do:

1. Ensure that all the bottle tops are clean.
2. Place all of the bottle tops flat side down on a hard surface (a surface that can take a few nail holes).
3. Hammer a hole in every single bottle top. An adult may need to do this bit.
4. Using the string, start with a smaller bottle top and help the children thread it through. Tie a knot and this will be the end of the snake.
5. Continue threading string through the bottle tops, trying to arrange them in similar sizes.
6. Once you are happy with the length, tie another knot.
7. The children can stick on googly eyes and create a tongue and the snake is ready. Pipe cleaners or sticks make great snake tongues, or you could cut scrap paper to the right shape for a more sustainable option.

*50 fantastic ideas for sustainability*